Sharnel Williams

I0159458

You are NOT Alone

Death-Grieving-Healing

Written By

Author Sharnel Williams

"You Are Not Alone"

sharnelwilliams@ymail.com

www.authorsharnel.com

www.facebook.com/sharnelw

www.twitter.com/AuthorSharnel

www.instagram.com/authorsharnel

www.blogtalkradio.com/authorsharnel

www.sharsheypublishingcompany.com

Sharnel Williams

<u>*Dedication*</u>

I want to first, thank God for giving me the strength to write another inspirational book.

To everyone, that has lost a loved one

A Mother, Father, Brother, Sister, Niece, Nephew, and/or Grandparent.

You Are Not Alone.

You will have good days and bad days.

We all have good memories of our loved ones, use them.

Time does heal

As long as you trust and believe in God, you will have the strength to live on.

*LIVE * LOVE * LIFE*

[3]

Death

What is death? We all have our own definition of what death means. According to Webster Dictionary death is defined as the act or fact of dying, loss, passing away, deceased, and bereavement. It is the State of being dead. Some people believe death is final while others believe there is an afterlife. No matter what our beliefs are we all deal with death differently.

In reality, we are all living to die. Death is a part of our everyday life. Every minute in the world someone dies. Is it fair that the people we love die? Do people like going to funerals? Can we stop death? The answer to each of these questions is no. We are all going to die at some point in our lives. We are told, and some of us believe that God has a plan for us all. He has a plan for us on earth, and He has a plan for us when we leave this earth. We don't know what the plan is, only the man upstairs knows. All we can do is live our lives to the fullest.

As humans, we spend too much worrying about material things and all of the nonsense. Once we are gone, we can't take the house, the car, the clothes, the money, or any other material things with us, so stop treasuring things we can't take with us. Start cherishing the people we will one day leave behind. Even though we can't take them with us, we can create memories.

The good thing about memories is no one can take away our memories, good or bad. Cameras are the best memory tool that has been invented for preserving one's memories. In our brain, we have plenty of memories of our loved ones, but a camera gives us a tangible picture to look at and reminisce. You can create many memories by using a camera and being active with those you love. You have to celebrate and observe life while you are on this earth. In the world today, there are cameras on cell phones, computers, and tablets. One snap and you have a picture that will last a lifetime. Life is short, but memories last a lifetime. You can even make videos of your loved ones and play them at a later date.

Spending time with loved ones is better than spending money on a loved one. Some people believe money is everything, but you can't take money with you once you are gone. Never take a love one for granted.

Tomorrow is not promised to anyone, and you can be gone in the wink of an eye. God did not promise us life, as a matter of fact, the only thing He promised us was death.

We love to play the blame game when things are not going right in our lives, and the first person we blame is God. We question Him a lot which we are not supposed to do if we have faith. Psalms 9:10 says, "And they that know your name will put their trust in you: for you, LORD, have not forsaken them that seek you." This means what it says, as long as we trust Him, He will not lead you astray.

Prayer changes things by giving our burdens to our higher power and leaving them there. Some of us only pray to the man above when some type of tragedy hits home. For example, many of us only donate blood when a family member or someone close to us is in need a blood transfusion. Stop waiting for a tragedy to hit home to call on God. If you knew God before a situation came into your life, you shouldn't have to question Him. He's shown up and showed out many times in your life prior to the tragedy so why question his authority.

Trust me, I know, I questioned him when my son passed away. I asked the infamous question, WHY? I questioned everyone when tragedy struck my life. I even questioned the things around me. As the years went by, I learned everything happens for a reason. We may inquire about the reason, but we will we never know the reason for why people die.

I have a quote I live by daily. I'm going to Live-Love-Life. I call it the three

L's. I think if everyone used the three L's, life would be much better for all of us. You have to have a reason to Live. You have to have a reason to Love. You have to have a reason to celebrate Life. Live, Love and enjoy Life. Without one how can you do the others? It's called the three L's not one or two L's. Life is what you make of it. You can be happy, or you can be sad. You can bring joy to your life, or you can be miserable. You have to take it one day at a time. The death of a loved one can break you in many ways such as not wanting to get out of bed, feelings of hopelessness, and developing depression, but it can also make you stronger.

Dealing with death is hard, but life does go on, and you will heal in time. Sometimes you may wonder does life actually goes on? Will my broken heart ever heal? The answer to both of these questions is yes! God will give you the strength to move on and Live*Love*Life again.

Everyone, at some point, has experienced the death of a close relative at some point in their life. When a loss such as this happens, it's hard to believe the person is actually gone. One of the first responses a person may have would be shock, especially if you didn't see it coming such as the cause of death being from a car accident. Sometimes God allows us to the opportunity to know when we are about to lose someone due to health issues and such. Only God knows how long we have to live on this earth. Doctors examine us, give us our test results and prescribe medication. Doctors play a big part in helping us get to the nature of our problem, but the only man who can really say when it's our time to leave this world is God.

We do different things every day in our life, except talk about death. We talk about it only when it happens. Death is so far from our minds in our everyday lives. We don't wake up with death on our mind. We don't go to sleep with death on our mind. I believe we shouldn't think about death. I wish we could live forever. You heard the saying we are born to die.

When our mothers first gave birth to us we were naked, toothless, some of us were balled, and we wore diapers. As you get older, things start to repeat itself. Your hair starts thinning out, you start losing your teeth, and you can't hold your urine which causes some to wear diapers. Do you understand the correlation between babies and our elderly? Once you pass away, all clothing is removed, and you are once again naked. This is history repeating itself.

You really have to love one another. If you haven't or don't speak to a family member, now is the time to reach out. Don't be mad, it's time to forgive. You can always forgive someone and put it behind you, it is not difficult. Once you forgive, you can't throw it back in that person's face later. Being able to forgive is one thing, and forgetting is another. Trust me, if you don't talk about your problems and something happens to the person you were mad at, you will live to regret it. Sometimes I hear people say, "I can never forgive her/him," yes, you can.

Trust me the death of a loved one changes everything.

Those who don't know my story, I'll share it. My son passed away from complications of leukemia at the age of 12. It was so hard for me. I went from stressing over his death to question myself. Why am I still here? What would I do without my son? I was lonely and thoughtless. I was one of those people that couldn't believe that God took my child away from me. I wanted answers, and nobody could give them to me. Yes, I blamed myself for doing something wrong, something that God didn't approve of. I went through losing a loved one that meant the world to me. My mind went crazy. I couldn't eat, talk, or think. What pulled me through was the fact that I had another son that needed me. Even though they were different in many ways, I still had one living son that needed me. I had to get myself together. I still had a child that I had to take care of. This wasn't like losing a parent because you get one mother and one father. God blessed me with two children, but one is no longer here. I know that he will always be a part of my heart. No, I didn't go to any support groups or counseling.

Therapy for me was turning my story into a book. I had to relive it like it had happened yesterday. I could not have done it without God giving me the strength to relive his death. I took it one day at a time and prayed a lot. I thought I was the only mother in the world that had lost a child. At that time, I just felt so alone, but reality kicked in before it was too late.

Family is very important. Stop taking them for granted and start showing them love. Death is death no matter how you look at it. Death is a fact of life.

Grieving

What is *Grief?*

Grieving -to feel or cause to feel grief, mournful, brokenhearted, sorrowful, and anguished. (Webster Dictionary)

Everyone grieves at some point in their life. It's a normal way to react to the loss of someone or something you love. Grief affects each person differently. People have physical and emotional reactions to grief which mainly occur after a loss. Losing someone is a process in life you will go through. Everyone has lost a loved one in their life.

What do you do after the death to pull through the grief stage? You will question everyone around you and ask why did this happened. You will be very emotional and stressed. Some people will cry and pace back and forth. Some may lose their appetite which causes them not to eat for days at a time. Some may even lock themselves in their room and just stare at the walls. You have to remember that God is with you, through bad and good times. Did you know that God will take you through different things and provide you different walks of life? Do not just pray when you are going through bad times. You have to pray through the good and bad times. God won't give you more than what you can handle.

There are so many ways you can grieve. Sometimes you might not even know you are grieving, but you are. Did you know that your *thoughts* after death are a part of grieving? It's a typical reaction, once a loved one or close friend passes away. What's the first thing you do when you find out a loved one has passed away? You begin to think. All sorts of things start running through your mind. For example, you start thinking about the person who died and your memories of that person. Sometimes you can become absent minded. Sometimes your mind will trick you into thinking you hear their voice. For some people, it's hard for them to process the person no longer being alive. All of us are different, and our reaction to death will vary.

Your *emotions* will be like a rollercoaster as you deal with your grief. You will feel angry at the person who died. You may feel sad, lonely, helpless, or hopeless. Remember, sometimes your emotions will make you vulnerable to certain things in your life. You will also feel angry at God, and you will question everyone around you. Some people feel relief from the death of a loved one. Especially, if the loved one was sick, and you didn't want them to suffer anymore. *Emotions* really start playing with your mind when the deceased and you were not on good terms. You may feel guilty or angry, wishing things could have been different. If only you could have said this or that. This type of thinking will constantly be on your mind. For this reason, I don't take anything or the people I love for granted. Once they are gone, they are not coming back. We as humans only have one life, and we must live it to the fullest. If someone in your family did something to you, and you stop speaking to that person, ask yourself, is it worth it? Once they close the door to the morgue, they will only reopen it to prepare that person for their funeral. You must tell your loved one how you feel before it's too late. It's just three little words. I Love You!

Did you know that *behavior* is part of the grieving process? Many people who are grieving have mood changes. One change is withdrawing from people. Meaning, you stop socializing and being around other people. You just don't feel like being bothered. Another *behavior* is not being able to sleep. You may toss and turn throughout the night. You may feel restless or wander aimlessly, forgetting what you were doing. You can also dream about the deceased frequently. A dream is defined by Webster Dictionary as a sequence of images, passing

through a sleeping person's mind. There will
be some good and bad dreams. When you
experience good dreams, don't ever let them
go. These dreams can be added to your
memoir of your deceased loved one.
Everyone dreams. Some people don't like to
talk about the dead and some do. Being able
to talk about your loved one can be a help in
the grieving process. I did this a lot. I would
also cry out of the blue. I would walk in the
kitchen, look up, and cry. I would scream
out. Why did it have to be my baby? I
consider crying as an *emotion* and *behavior*.

Did you know going through
something *physical* is a part of grieving?
Once you learn a loved one or close friend
has passed away, your physical being starts
to react to the grief. People can display
physical behaviors after a loved one has

passed. You can feel weak and exhausted from all of the confusion you are going through. Medically there is nothing wrong with you. It's your mind getting the best of you. It feels like your body has separated from your brain has developed a mind of its own. Your nerves tend to be weak. You may have shortness of breath or a dry mouth. Some may have anxiety or experience a tightness in the chest and throat. Some people may have problems with their stomach, such as a queasy or nauseated feeling.

Thoughts of your loved one could consume your every waking thought. You may ask yourself questions about it the death as if there was really an answer to your questions. We all think about the whys and what ifs. What if he/she was still here?

What would I say or do? What if, we would have known sooner? What if, we could have seen the signs/symptoms early? What if, what if, what if. We let our minds get the best of us. There is no answer to the, what ifs because we will never know. We will never know because that person is no longer alive. Feeling overwhelmed is normal in this situation.

There are so many more reactions people go through. For example, *Denial*, *Vulnerability*, *Depression* and *Acceptance*.

Have you ever been in *Denial*? It is a typical reaction to overwhelming *emotions*. Denial of the death helps protect the mind from overwhelming emotions you may not be ready to deal with at that moment. How many times have you been told that someone has passed away and responded by saying, "No"? I can say I was in *denial* during my situation.

No one wants to believe their loved one has passed away. Everyone goes through this temporary reaction. I call it a temporary situation because it is. This process doesn't last forever. Each day it gets easier to move on with your life while holding your loved one's memory in your heart.

Have you ever been *Vulnerable*? Vulnerability can be a reaction to death as well. Anyone can be *Vulnerable, and it has nothing to do with someone dying.* You can get attacked, hurt by someone, criticized, tempted, or influenced by others, and this causes you to do things that are out of your character.

There are so many things we as humans grieve about such as a broken relationship, a divorce, loss of a pet, loss of a job, etc. You would be surprised what people grieve over. When most people mourn, they're not just grieving over the loss of a loved one, especially if they had advanced notice of the impending death. Some people use this as the time to grieve for everything they have ever lost. The loss of a loved one can be a profoundly painful experience. The grief that follows may permeate everything, making it hard to eat, sleep, or have much of an interest in the life going on around you.

Did you know there is something called *Healthy Grieving?* You must drink lots of water. Dehydration and build-up of toxins will make you feel worse. It is also important to exhale and inhale. Your breathing pattern is paramount and, for this reason, you must take breathing breaks. Resting is good for when you are grieving. I call it calming down and relaxing. It helps to deal with stress. Multivitamins can also play a big part in helping you grieve in a healthy manner. They provide needed nutrients to the body and enhance the foods you eat.

Walking can help you to relax too. Some people like running or jogging through the park. Yoga and meditation are good for the body. Find ways to exercise your body so your mind is not consumed with your loss.

We can all start grieving in healthier ways and take care of our body while doing it. I know we all grieve differently, but we all cry the same. We all get advice from others. Some may have gone through the same thing, and some may have no clue what is going on. This is when you can step in and share your story of overcoming the loss. You can listen to everyone, but most importantly listen to yourself. In a situation like this, people shut other people out. I think you should reach out to others, open up and talk about it. Once the heaviness is lifted from your shoulders, you will feel lighter. I've been there, everything I'm writing about I know for a fact. Try not to worry so much and focus on one thing instead of five things at a time.

Once you begin to open up and share your story, keep going. Don't allow yourself to return to that dark place. Take it one day at a time. If you are a woman, call your girls up and make it a ladies' night out. If you are a man, call your boys up and go out on the town. The problem will still be there, but it will be a little less hard to bear. You just have to put it to the side and enjoy yourself. There's nothing wrong with getting back on track, once you lose a loved one. You may feel guilty, but take a moment to look in the mirror and ask yourself, why am I feeling guilty? Would your love one want you to stay in your room, miserable staring at four walls? I know my son is proud of me. He's looking down on me and saying *Live*Love*Life* Mom.*

I really believe things happen for a reason. Take a look at where you were at once upon a time to how far you have come today. Sometimes you have to lose something to get to your future. If God has to take someone out of your life, so you can be where you are today, you should be thanking God.

People, places, and things are not with you forever. There is no such thing as forever. They are put in our life for a reason and season. Everything expires around us. Nothing is promised to us. You have to trust and believe in God, and don't question what He does. I know it's hard, it was hard for me. I learned never to question the man above. People naturally prefer to blame others and question something they'll never get an answer for when it comes to death.

I learned to get involved and listen to others when they are grieving. Some people just want an ear to listen as they share their thoughts. In time you will heal, there's no time frame to heal as we all heal in our own way. You may grieve for days, weeks, months, or even years, you can't place a time frame for your grief. There is no magic pill for grieving. You won't wake up one day and say, *today I am not grieving.* What you should say instead is, *I will try not to think about the death of my loved one today.* Remember your emotions are working overtime.

Grief consists of more than your feelings. You may hear people telling you, "Everything will be okay" or "You have to be strong!" or "Time will heal!" or "You have to get on with your life!" which all sounds good if it was that easy. It's important for you to be clear that this is your time to grieve, not theirs. People can't tell you how to grieve. Everyone grieves differently.

Death forces us to look for a deeper purpose in life.

Healing

What is *Healing*?

Healing- To make or become well, curing, therapy, remedial and medicine. (Webster Dictionary)

Now that you have an understanding of the grief process, it is time to work on healing. I know you may be wondering if healing is possible, and I want to confirm that it is. We have to take steps to heal, just like we had to take steps in dealing with grief and death.

By talking to others who are grieving, you can find a healthy outlet for your thoughts and feelings amongst people who may be having similar experiences. I didn't go to a support group. I thought it wasn't for me at the time. What works for some doesn't work for others but do not allow other people's experiences to hinder you from experiencing what a support group can offer. Just because I felt it wouldn't work for me, doesn't mean it's not going to work for you. To each his own. You can find support groups in your area by checking with your local hospitals, religious groups, counseling centers, and hospice facilities. You may even find someone who hosts private support groups in their homes. This offers an atmosphere conducive to healing. Yes, a lot of people gather in their homes and talk about their experiences with others and learn ways to cope with death in a healthy manner. I have talked to people who have attended support groups, and it seemed to work for some of them. Everyone has a different experience. Through my grief process, I learned that it is good to talk to people. You should never hold anything bottled up inside of you. That is not healthy. You could explode at the wrong time due to the bottled up feelings you may have, and that can be a dangerous situation. I didn't open up at first, but I learned not to hold anything inside. I didn't go to any support groups or counseling. I wanted to talk to someone who actually knew what I had been through. I wanted that person to feel my pain and understand it. In my case, I wanted to talk to another mother who had lost a child. Anyone can say they understand, but how do they really know if they have never lost a child of their own. From my point of view, you would never understand what a person is going through unless you have walked in that person's shoes. Some people would like to help you through this time, but do they really know how? Sometimes you may just want someone to listen to someone talk without responding and at other times you may want to do all of the talking. Always do what you feel is best for you. Only you know what is best for you. I say this because stress can take a toll on your body.

I know it's hard to continue doing what you were doing before the tragedy hit. Just remember to take care of your health by eating right, drinking plenty of water, exercise daily, and get plenty of rest.

Death is not the only loss we heal from. We recover from life circumstances on a daily basis which makes us stronger people. Think about a break up you experienced in the past. How much time did it take for you to heal and return to your daily life? What about from being sick or having a surgery. The doctors give you instructions to follow, and they give you an indirect time frame in which it may take you to heal, but they never give you an exact date. Healing is a process that takes time.

Learning to adjust and live without a loved one can be hard. Especially, if you don't have anyone to turn too. Death is not like a 24-hour bug; you won't get well overnight.

One way that may help you to heal is keeping some of your loved one's personal items, like a piece of clothing or jewelry to reflect upon. Others things such as their favorite song, movie, or restaurant can be a part of your healing process and provide you with good memories to think about and share with others.

Having hobbies can help you to heal as well. It is a good idea to get back into the things you love doing. I know it will be the last thing on your mind, but it will be one of the healthier things you can do to help speed up your recovery time. I'm not saying jump right back into it, go slow and work your way back into it because it does work. Keeping yourself busy will be a huge help in the process.

There are plenty of books about healing. If you are having a difficult time with your grieving process, I think you should talk to your doctor, so he/she can give you advice on what to do next. Like I said, everyone is different, some might need medicine to relax and stay calm. A day of relaxation and massage at a spa or a weekend can do wonders for you in your time of need.

Children are affected by death just like adults. However, they are not equipped with the same experiences. When talking to kids about death you should be honest. They may not understand the meaning of death, or they may feel a sense of responsibility for the death. When my son passed away, my oldest was eighteen-years-old. I didn't know how to discuss it with him, and he was eighteen. You look at your children as still being kids no matter what age they are. Children are the most vulnerable when it comes to death. That's why it's so important to be honest with them. They have to heal too. You have to make sure the child knows he or she is not responsible for the death. They may have questions and want to discuss their thoughts and feelings, they may not. Let them know you are there for them and they can ask you anything. Let them know it's alright to be angry and crying helps to release their feelings. Children have the same feelings as adults. Adults have a better understanding of death. Sometimes a child may need to talk to a counselor or attend a support group geared towards children. They may even need medicine to help them to relax. We all have to cope with death in our lifetime, no matter how old you are.

What is *Distraction*?

Distraction- Anything that distracts confusingly or amusingly diversion, great mental distress (Webster Dictionary).

Yes, distraction can be a part of healing. Plus, you will be amazed at how well it works. My doctor thought it was best that she sent me back to work. I truly didn't believe it would work, but it did. I had to call my doctor and thank her for sending me back to work. I had so many distractions at work. I didn't have time to concentrate on my son passing away. I was doing other things and didn't have time to sit around and think. Not only did going back to work help, getting out of the house was a distraction. It is so important to get back into your usual routine, and I encourage everyone who is going through the grieving process to get back to the lives they led prior to the death.

Slowly, get back into doing your normal activities. Trust me, "*You Are Not Alone*".

Helping others with a death of a loved one.

There are many ways you can help others who have lost a loved one. You don't have to hold a conversation all the time. Sometimes people don't feel like talking about their loss. It may be too soon for that person. You can help in other ways such as picking up groceries, cooking a meal, or volunteering to keep other children in the family to give the parents a break. It's hard going through the death of a loved one with kids running around the house. You can run errands, like going to the post office or picking the kids up from school. You can even clean the house for them. There are many things you can do to help others. They will appreciate you, and they will never forget you being there for them. People who are grieving may not reach out to you because they are so consumed with their loss which means you will need to reach out to them. You don't have to ask can you help, like Nike said, "Just Do It". Make a phone call or just stop by their home. Try not to force them to talk or hold a conversation about the death of their loved one. When they are ready to talk about it, they will open up to you. You can also send a sympathy card to let them know you are thinking about them. Every hand is a helping hand.

Sharing & telling your story

Tell your story! At first, is will be hard to do. Your emotions will get the best of you in the beginning. You have to say to yourself that you are not responsible for the death of your loved one, and you are not the only one on this earth who has lost a loved one. Even though it may seem that you are the only person in the world that is going through a loss, just remember *"You Are Not Alone"*.

Find affirmations that will make you feel better. For example, my loved one would want me to be happy and to continue to live my life, my love one is looking down on me, and he/she is proud of me, my loved one will want me to tell this story so it can inspire others, or I will share my joy and sorrows with others. Tell your story when you are ready to tell it.

Keep God first in your life. Praying will get you through this as long as you

believe and have faith. Things happen for a
reason, and people are in our life for only a
season. God sends them to us for different
reasons. Their purpose could be to give us
messages, teach us something we need to
learn, or to fill a void in our lives. We don't
know why God brings people into our lives.
God has a plan for everyone on this earth.
We have to live life to the fullest and don't
take anyone for granted.

Once I was able to tell my story, I felt
so much better. Trust me, it took years for
me to become comfortable with talking
about it. I've only been talking about it for
the past couple of years. I couldn't talk
because the memory was too fresh for me. I
would cry every time I thought about my
son. I think what helped me get through this
period in my life was writing and telling my

story in a book first. Remember, I didn't go to a support group or counselor. With the strength, God gave me and the trust I have for Him, I was able to write my story. Yes, it was hard. I stopped a couple of times. I cried and repeatedly told myself I couldn't do it. I was wrong. We can do anything we put our minds to and I'm living proof. You will have feelings of being overwhelmed, but you have to do what you have to do.

My son meant the world to me, and a piece of my heart will never be replaced. You can't replace the death of a loved one. People ask me how I survived this devastating loss. I always tell them, God helped me. I heard so many stories about parents who have lost a child and sometimes they got lost in the process. I consider myself blessed. I didn't have to take any medication, and I didn't turn to alcohol or do any type of drugs. I told myself there was a reason God took my son at the age of twelve-years-old. He had decided it was time for my son to be his angel. I don't know the reason my son was picked, but my guess is to spread the word about leukemia and tell our story to help others pull through the loss of a loved one, especially a child.

I still have questions, and I still have my moments which I will always have in my mind. There's nothing I can do except continue to pray about it. I'm still healing and making progress daily in coming to terms with my loss. A year after my son's death, I started talking to my husband about having another baby. I know now it was the hurt and pain I was going through at the time. I needed comfort, and I was choosing another child to get that comfort. Knowing what I know now, a child can't be replaced by another child. God works in mysterious ways, instead of having a child of my own, He gave me a grandson to raise. Things changed once my grandson entered my life. I have Christmas and a smile once again. I know that I'm blessed, and I know that time heals all. I am living proof.

*LIVE*LOVE*LIFE*

Check out my book!

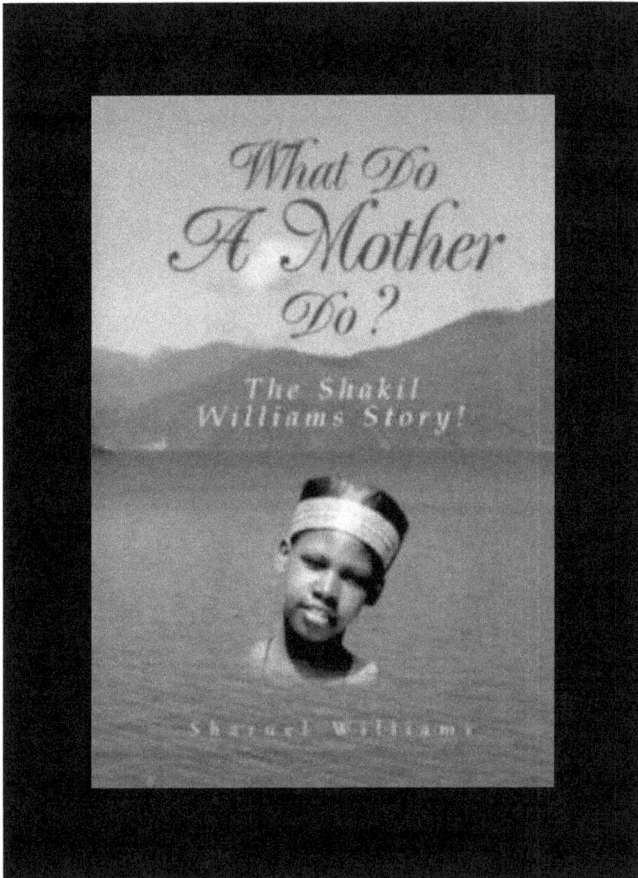

You Are Not Alone

Sharnel Williams